Vegetable Bliss

Simple Seed-to-Table Inspiration

JULIE SOCHACKI

Graphics by Jason Houston

BALBOA.
PRESS

A DIVISION OF HAY HOUSE

ISBN: 978-1-4525-5426-6 (sc)
ISBN: 978-1-4525-5425-9 (e)

Library of Congress Control Number: 2012910248

Balboa Press books may be ordered through booksellers or by contacting:

Balboa Press
A Division of Hay House
1663 Liberty Drive
Bloomington, IN 47403
www.balboapress.com
1-(877) 407-4847

Because of the dynamic nature of the Internet, any web addresses or links contained in this book may have changed since publication and may no longer be valid. The views expressed in this work are solely those of the author and do not necessarily reflect the views of the publisher, and the publisher hereby disclaims any responsibility for them.

The author of this book does not dispense medical advice or prescribe the use of any technique as a form of treatment for physical, emotional, or medical problems without the advice of a physician, either directly or indirectly. The intent of the author is only to offer information of a general nature to help you in your quest for emotional and spiritual well-being. In the event you use any of the information in this book for yourself, which is your constitutional right, the author and the publisher assume no responsibility for your actions.

Printed in the United States of America

Balboa Press rev. date: 06/29/2012

For community supported farmers and their members.
Thank you for up-holding the highest vision of a local and
sustainable food system and actually living it on a daily basis.

"I wake up each morning torn between a desire to save the world and a desire to savor the world. This makes it very hard to plan the day."

— E. B. White

Contents

These recipes call for simplicity and intuition, so please make them your own. They are the basis for many variations. Although in their current form they are plant-based, as the cook your dietary and taste preferences will guide you to add dairy, wheat, and animal protein when appropriate.

In a world of fast food and quick-paced lifestyles, these recipes ask you to slow down, listen to your senses, and create delicious vegetable dishes without heavy sauces, complicated ingredients or several, difficult steps. Instead, the vegetables in this book are prepared simply and deliciously, letting the flavors of the vegetables shine through and allowing you to savor them in their natural beauty.

Simple and fresh cooking starts with maximizing the deep flavors of the vegetables with simple ingredients such as lemons, limes, fresh herbs, garlic, ginger, extra virgin olive oil, nut oils and sea salt, just to name a few. The recipes in *Vegetable Bliss* use these ingredients with delicious results.

The "bliss" is found in the slowing down. Visiting a local farm or working your own garden, returning to your kitchen with a basket of local, fresh veggies, and preparing them simply to share with others reconnects us to our roots, to our Mother Earth and to our community.

Our vegetable gardens and local farms hold the keys to our health. The vitamins, minerals and nutrients found in freshly grown vegetables can't be matched through alternative means, so please join me on a culinary adventure, as you prepare simple and delicious vegetable recipes all year long. Share your veggie creations and spread the word that vegetables are one of our greatest blessings!

Wishing you a life filled with simple pleasures,

Julie Sochacki

Acknowledgements

Thank you to Lerae Gidyk for getting me to this place of magic and miracles where all of my dreams come true.

Thank you to Jason Houston, a creative genius and incredible photographer. Meeting him eight years ago was a blessing and working with him is a breeze.

Thanks to all of the farms for constantly sending me tips and ideas. I am grateful for you all!

Thank you to Katrina Kenison whose brilliant and authentic writings allowed me to slow down and enjoy all of those ordinary days and to Cheryl Richardson who introduced me to the importance of self-care and to the power of grace in my life.

Thank you to all of the women (too many to name, but you know who you are . . . wink) who have inspired me along my path.

Thank you to my mother, grandmother and aunts for instilling a love of cooking in me at a young age.

Thank you to my father for introducing me to the beauty, wonder and magnificence of nature.

Thank you to Chris, Brandon and Sean, my three loves.

Simple Solutions

Fast, fresh, fantastic ways to use your veggies now!

Community farms from across the United States joined together to share their best veggie tips. Many vegetables are listed along with quick and delicious recipes and ideas of what you can do with your veggies NOW!

ENJOYING EVERY LAST BITE—
Before you bring in the new veggies, use the veggies in your fridge.

Try doing this with the end of your weekly share:

If you want to crisp up cucumbers, summer squash, carrots or other root veggies, simply put them in a bowl of cold water in the fridge for a couple hours.

Avalon Acres Farms
Hohenwald, Tennessee

What do you do with left-over veggies?

GRATE! Grate veggies in soups, stews, stir-fries, and quick pasta or rice dishes.

BLEND! Blend them in a smoothie. Make pesto.

PUREE! Pour pureed squash, cauliflower or broccoli into soup to thicken it!

WRAP! Mix veggies with a light vinaigrette and wrap them in a corn tortilla or other wrap.

JULIENNE! Julienne veggies, coat with olive oil and sea salt, bake at 400 degrees F until crisp.

PICKLE! Preserve the harvest and pickle extra veggies.

Asparagus

Blanch and pair with a dipping sauce such as a pesto for a quick snack.

Create a delicious soup such as "creamy" asparagus soup or add chopped to any veggie soup.

Grill and add to a salad!

The absolute best way to prepare asparagus is to roast it. Cut the ends off and lay them in a single layer on a cookie sheet. Drizzle with olive oil and sprinkle with salt and pepper if you like. Put in a 400 degree F oven for about 7-10 minutes until tender when pierced with a fork. Amazing!

Crazy Boy Farm
Rush City, Minnesota

Beets

Boil, peel, cool and mix with chopped red onion and vinaigrette.

Roast with sweet potatoes and leeks for a substantial and colorful side dish.

Freshly dug beets will keep for months—not washed—in the refrigerator.

The flavor of beets varies with age and size, almost more than for any other vegetable. Very young ones, especially thinnings from a row, can be eaten, greens and all, with their well-scrubbed skins left on after cooking—roasted, sautéed or grilled.

Easy Sautéed Beet Greens:

Cut leaves from stalks and slice into 1/4-inch strips. Sauté 3 packed cups of strips in 2 tablespoons of walnut oil. For 1 to 2 minutes, stir with a wooden spoon, scraping the strips against the bottom and sides of the skillet. Turn heat to low and cook for 5 minutes. Serve with a splash of sherry or cider vinegar.

Lakes and Valley CSA
Park Rapids, Minnesota

Every year during week two Bird's Haven Farms in Ohio has the "Great Beet Challenge." There are always foods new CSA members think they "hate" or remember from childhood. Most common is the pickled beet from their childhood!

The farm gives the following recipe and tells every member they "MUST" try it—just once!! The members always come back and realize they LOVE beets and are more willing to try all future vegetables. Remember that "farm fresh" is different than products from the grocery store, especially canned beets!

ROASTED BEETS

Everyone remembers their Grandmother's pickled beets, but have you tried fresh market baked beets? No matter how much you "think" you don't like beets, this recipe will prove you wrong!

1 pound medium fresh beets, peeled
4 teaspoons olive oil
1/2 teaspoon kosher salt
3 sprigs fresh rosemary

Cut each beet into six wedges; place in a large re-sealable plastic bag. Add olive oil and salt; seal and shake to coat. Place a piece of heavy-duty foil (about 12 inches long) in a 15-in. x 10-in. x 1-in. baking pan. Arrange beets on foil and top with rosemary. Fold foil around beet mixture and seal tightly. Bake at 400 degrees F for 1-1/4 to 1-1/2 hours or until beets are tender. Discard rosemary sprigs.

Bird's Haven Farms
Granville, Ohio

Broccoli and Cauliflower

Cut, wash, and serve with a dip such as hummus.

Enjoy a broccoli salad on a hot day.

Add roasted broccoli and cauliflower to your holiday menu.

Farmer John Peterson, author of *The Real Dirt on Vegetables*, has some great tips on cauliflower.

Cauliflower is the mildest member of the brassica family. Like its cousin broccoli, cauliflower is actually a mass of unopened flower buds that would burst into edible yellow flowers if allowed to mature. Hiding its head demurely within a bonnet of furled leaves, cauliflower stays tender and maintains a white or creamy color. In spots where the leaves uncurl a little early, the sun turns the cauliflower slightly yellow or brown.

Storage

Wrap dry, unwashed cauliflower loosely in plastic and store it in the refrigerator. It will keep for up to a week but is sweetest if used within a few days.

Handling

Trim off the leaves and any brown spots. Rinse the cauliflower and cut out the cone-shaped core at the base using a small paring knife. Stop there if you plan to cook it whole. Otherwise, proceed to break it into florets or chop.

John Peterson
Angelic Organics
Caledonia, Illinois

Brussels Sprouts

Remove base and any wilted leaves; wash the Brussels sprouts in bowl of water. Soak in lemon juice and water mixture to detect and remove any worms. Blanch for about three minutes, cool and freeze.

Make lemon-walnut or garlic-infused Brussels sprouts!

Simply roast some Brussels sprouts with olive oil and sea salt. Bake at 400 degrees F until brown and tender.

Sauté a chopped onion in extra virgin olive oil. Add fresh ginger, salt, pepper and ½ cup pistachios. Add Brussels Spouts and cook for five minutes longer.

Jones Farm
Chelmsford, MA

Cabbage

Make Asian Slaw at your next get-together.

Red Cabbage, German Style is perfect for a holiday!

Cabbage can be stored for many months in the refrigerator. Before storing remove as few leaves as possible as these help protect the cabbage. Cabbages can be held in the field for a long time. To prevent them from cracking because of getting too big or absorbing too much water, take a spade shovel and cut off half of the roots at the base of the cabbage.

North Creek Community Farm
Prairie Farm, Wisconsin

Carrots

Wash, peel and crunch on a carrot from the garden.
Add to smoothies.
Pair with a dip such as pesto or hummus.
Add to soups and stews.
Make Easiest Carrots for a weeknight dinner or for a holiday side dish.

Braise whole small carrots or halved large carrots in butter or olive oil, a little water or stock, and a bit of honey and Dijon mustard. Braise until tender and then let the liquid reduce to a syrupy, sweet-tangy glaze.

Roast carrots, alone or with other root vegetables. Lightly coat in olive oil and season with salt, pepper, cumin, and a pinch of cayenne in a medium-hot oven until tender and caramelized.

Boistfort Valley Farm
Cutis, Washington

Celeriac

STORAGE — Celeriac can be stored for a long time. We keep it in our coolers at the farm for about 4 months throughout the winter without any loss of quality, and the same can be done in the produce drawer of your fridge. Wrap it loosely in a plastic bag to help retain its moisture if you're storing it over a month.

WASH/CLEAN/PEEL — Celeriac can look scary if you're trying to prepare it for the first time. The outside is rough and uneven. We recommend peeling the outside skin with a good quality vegetable peeler or pairing knife. Once removed, the flesh is firm and easy to slice or chop as needed for your recipe.

PREPARATION — One of the best and simplest ways to enjoy celeriac is in a mash with potatoes. We recommend a ratio of 2:1, potatoes to celeriac. Boil or steam the celeriac and potatoes until soft and then mash together with your choice of butter or olive oil and salt and pepper to taste. Celeriac is also delicious diced in a wide variety of soups (it gives your soup an earthy, celery flavor) or even roasted in the oven with olive oil and salt & pepper.

Golden Earthworm Organic Farm
Jamesport, New York

Choi

Chinese cabbage is so versatile. Also called choi, bok choy, pak choi, bok choi, and pak choy.

Just wash and chop! Sauté choi and enjoy as a side dish. Chop the leaves and stems and toss them into a salad or stir fry!

Choi Stir Fry

8 cups cleaned choi (leaves and stalks separated)
1 1/2 tablespoons peanut oil
1 garlic clove, sliced thinly
1/4 inch slice of fresh ginger, minced
1 teaspoon soy sauce

Chop the leaves and stalks into one-inch pieces. Heat a large skillet to medium high and add the oil. Cook the stems in the oil, stirring often, for four minutes or until softened. Next, add garlic, ginger and soy sauce and the chopped leaves. Cook for two minutes more, stirring and tossing often.

Cooking Greens

When asking community-supported farm members which veggies in their weekly baskets overwhelm them the most, they say cooking greens. This is because they need to be cleaned and stored, and then finally eaten, but how? Provident Organic Farm in Maryland gives us a simple, practical approach to storing, washing and preparing greens. Once the greens are cleaned and stored, read below for some simple and delicious ways to prepare greens!

From smoothies and chips to pesto and a super quick and yummy side dish, you will be smiling as you collect your weekly greens!

All About Greens

Greens come in different shapes, sizes and flavors, but they all have one thing in common—they are largely composed of water. They are easy to keep fresh and delicious once you know the simple basics of handling and storing. Since most greens are grown in sandy soil, they require a bit more care in washing to remove the extra grit. Greens must be washed before eating or cooking.

Store

All greens prefer a cool, moist (but not wet) environment. Store sturdier greens like kale and mustards loosely wrapped in plastic or vegetable storage bags in the crisper section of the refrigerator. The crisper section has high humidity, so vegetables should last a little bit longer when stored there. For lettuce, invest in a salad spinner. You will not regret it! Look for one with a bowl, spinner top and internal basket (avoid spinners with drainage holes). Lettuce may be stored unwashed, but it is easy to wash and store right in the spinner, ready to eat at a moment's notice.

Wash

With the exception of lettuce greens, do not wash greens until just before using. This wash method seems tedious, but the extra few minutes is worth it to avoid crunching down on a mouthful of grit and sand: Fill a tub or bucket with cool water. Separate the head of greens into leaves and swish around in the water. Hold leaves against the side of the tub and wait for the grit to settle at the bottom. Discard water (good for watering house plants). Repeat at least another time or two until no grit settles at the bottom of the tub.

Prepare

The greens from farmer's markets, community supported farms and gardens are so fresh and tender that stems can be eaten along with the leaves. If you do not like stems or if they seem a bit tough, remove them: fold the leaf in half lengthwise along the stem. Hold the stem firmly in one hand and tear the leaves off with the other hand. Leaves of sturdier greens may be left whole, torn or cut into strips for cooking. Lettuce will stay crisp longer and hold up to dressings better when leaves are torn rather than cut.

REMINDER! Uproot Farm from Princeton, MN shares a special note about de-stemming kale:

Hold a leaf by the stem upside down in your hand. Cupping the thumb and index finger of your free hand around the top of the stem, pull downward in one quick, smooth motion, tearing the leaf away from the stem as you go.

Try these four fast and delicious ways to use greens. From breakfast to dinner, greens are versatile and super healthy!

Blue and Green Smoothie

I love to add just-picked greens to a smoothie!

My favorite is a blueberry-greens smoothie, which is not only packed with tons of vitamins and nutrients, but has anti-inflammatory properties as well.

1 cup blueberries, frozen
1 handful fresh greens, about one cup, washed well
½ banana, peeled and frozen
1 tablespoon of nut butter or sun butter (I like walnut or almond)
1 cup of ice water
4 ice cubes

Blend all and enjoy! What a way to start your day!

Kale Chips

Yes, it's this easy! Eat these as a snack or sprinkle on soup, salad or veggie side dishes for a salty crunch!

1 head of kale, ribs removed, cut into 2 inch pieces
2 tablespoons olive oil
Sea salt

Preheat oven to 350 degrees F. Wash kale in salad spinner, dry well and cut into bite-sized pieces. Toss kale with olive oil and salt. Place on a cookie sheet and bake until crisp, about 10-15 minutes or until slightly browned, turning once. Cool and store in an air-tight container.

McKinley Community CSA
an urban CSA located in the McKinley Neighborhood of North Minneapolis

Winter Pesto

Top a baked sweet potato with this Omega-3-packed pesto; the bitter pesto and the sweet potato are the perfect pairing!

Place these ingredients in a blender:

1 shallot, chopped
1/4 cup extra virgin olive oil
1/2 cup organic veggie broth
1/2 cup walnuts, chopped
3 cups of any combo of arugula, chard, flat leaf parsley or winter greens

Blend until you reach a pesto-like consistency. If too thin add more greens and if too difficult to blend, add more veggie broth.

Use as a spread on sandwiches, with crackers or tortillas, in mashed potatoes or on baked sweet potatoes, as a topping for bean soup, or simply combine with cooked wheat-free pasta!

Sautéed Greens

Toss these garlicky greens with pasta or serve over brown rice for a more substantial meal!

3 tablespoons of extra virgin olive oil
4 medium garlic cloves, minced
2 pounds of Swiss chard, kale or other hearty greens, stem ends discarded and washed well but not dried
Sea salt and freshly ground pepper

In a large pan heat oil over medium heat, add garlic and cook for one minute. Add greens, reduce heat, cover and cook about 5 minutes or until leaves are wilted. Season with salt and pepper.

Cucumbers

Create your own cucumber salad!

Make pickles!

Add sliced cucumber to a large glass of cold water for a refreshing summer drink.

Add diced cucumbers to a salsa. Cucumbers balance hot peppers really well!

We grow so many cucumbers and none go to waste. Many of us are on cleansing diets, and we add half of a sliced cucumber to a quart of water, along with some mint leaves and half of a lemon. It makes it easier to drink tons of water every day, as it tastes so refreshing, plus it helps cleanse the body.

Sunset View Farm CSA
Andover Twp, New Jersey

Daikon Radishes

Daikon radish is the overwhelming underdog of the Community Supported Agriculture (CSA) farm. Without substantial sugar content, flashy appearance, and a traditional holiday to stand by, the odds seem stacked against any small chance for the daikon's acceptance in today's CSA! We've mentioned the reverence with which the Japanese culture holds the daikon, and that it's a fabulous source of vitamin C, potassium, and folic acid. Please, for the love of vegetables, give the daikon a chance and eat it. If not for your health, do it for the farm staff!

Braised Daikon

1 1/2 pounds fresh daikon, peeled and diced
2 tablespoons light cooking oil
1 teaspoon sugar
1 1/2 tablespoons tamari (gluten-free)

Put daikon in saucepan, cover with water, and boil for 5 minutes. Drain well. Heat skillet, add oil, cover, and bring to boil. Reduce heat to medium-low and cook, stirring occasionally, until daikon is tender but not mushy, about 20 minutes. Add sugar and tamari, cook 3 minutes longer. Serve hot.

Daikon and Carrot Slaw

8 ounces daikon (Japanese white radish), peeled, cut into 1-inch pieces (about 1/2 large)
6 ounces peeled baby carrots
1 cup chopped green onions
1/3 cup seasoned rice vinegar
2 1/2 tablespoons minced peeled fresh ginger
1 1/2 tablespoons Asian sesame oil
1 1/2 teaspoons chili-garlic sauce

Fit processor with large-hole grating disk. Working with a few pieces at a time, push daikon and carrots through feed tube until all vegetables are grated. Transfer vegetables to medium bowl. Add green onions. Whisk vinegar, ginger, oil, and chili-garlic sauce in small bowl to blend. Pour over vegetables and toss to coat. Season with salt and serve.

The Food Project—Lincoln
Lincoln, Massachusetts

Eggplant

Grill eggplant and top on a salad or use in a wrap.

Create a delicious eggplant caviar dip.

Store on countertop at a cool room temperature or keep in hydrator drawer in refrigerator for up to a week. For long-term storage, dishes like ratatouille freeze well in airtight containers.

Farmer Joe's Gardens
Wallingford, Connecticut

Fennel

Fennel is completely edible, the bulb, the stems, the leaves, and the seed! The bulb can be cored, sliced, and eaten raw, stir-fried, sautéed, or simmered in soups, sauces, or curries. The stems can be chopped up and cooked in soups or stocks, or peeled then sliced and eaten raw. The leaves are nice in salads, soups, or as a garnish.

For a very simple salad, whisk together 1 part white wine vinegar with 2 parts olive oil, some salt and freshly ground pepper. Add very thinly sliced fennel bulb and peeled and sliced bottom of fennel stem and toss to combine. Garnish with fennel leaf and serve.

Driftless Organics
Soldiers Grove, Wisconsin

Fennel: A sweet and crisp licorice-scented vegetable.

To store: Only the bottom white bulb is edible (top green stalks and fronds are too fibrous, although they can be used to make vegetable stocks if you don't mind the licorice background), so trim off the stalks and store just the bulb, wrapped in a plastic bag in the vegetable drawer to keep it crisp. Compost the stalks.

To eat: Wonderful both raw and cooked. For a raw treat, think crudité or thinly sliced in salads. To cook, use in long braised meat dishes, so it melts into tenderness, or try cutting in 1-inch wedges through the core (so it stays in tact), toss with olive oil, and roast, alone or with other vegetables like small halved potatoes until caramelized. (30 minutes at 375 degrees F usually does the trick).

Common Ground Farm
Beacon, New York

Fiddlehead Ferns

These mild veggies with an asparagus-like flavor are only in season for a few weeks. Sauté ferns with olive oil, fresh garlic and any herbs you have on-hand. These ferns are high in alpha-carotene, which is linked to longevity!

Garlic

Sleepy Root Farm in Howard Lake, Minnesota on Garlic Scapes:

Garlic scapes are a highly coveted item on our farm. They are the flowering stems of garlic plants, often discarded by larger garlic operations. They can be chopped and added to soups and dishes just as you normally would garlic, but in many ways garlic scapes are more versatile than its bulb counterpart as a main attraction. Scapes are wonderful marinated with a little olive oil or a teriyaki sauce and grilled. My favorite way to prepare them is using a food processor to make a scape pesto or spread. Process scapes with olive oil and a little salt to make an easy, garlicky spread—add some Parmesan cheese, if desired, and nuts (almond or pine nuts are my favorite) to make a heartier pesto. Either one can be frozen in ice cube trays for easy use or spread thinly between parchment paper and freeze, making it easy to break off small chunks when needed. This beautiful flowering stalk has a short season, so enjoy while you can!

Garlic Scape Dip

Garlic is our niche crop on our farm, and this is a well-used recipe!

½ cup finely minced garlic scapes
1 tablespoon finely minced basil leaves
2 cups sour cream (or alternately plain coconut yogurt, highly recommended!)
Sea salt and freshly ground pepper to taste

Mix together in a bowl and serve with veggies such as carrots, broccoli, sweet peppers, zucchini or cucumbers.

Josie Porter Farm
Stroudsburg, Pennsylvania

Roasted Garlic

4 heads of garlic
4 tablespoons of olive oil
Sea salt and freshly ground pepper

Preheat oven to 400 degrees F. Slice off the top quarter inch of each garlic head. Place on tin foil. Brush olive oil and sprinkle salt and pepper on garlic heads. Wrap in tin foil and place in hot oven. Roast 35 minutes or until garlic is soft. Squeeze into mashed potatoes, add to a green salad, or spread on a wrap.

Garlic-rubbed Salad

Mash 2-3 garlic cloves and rub them all around a ceramic or wooden bowl. Put spinach or mixed greens in the bowl and stir thoroughly with a bit of olive oil (important to apply first), balsamic vinegar, and a hint of sea salt, then any other herbs as desired. Viola! You have a delicious and dynamic salad with layers of flavor and minimal work.

Featherstone Farm
Rushford, Minnesota

Green Beans

Lightly steam until bright green and still crispy, not overcooked, or green beans will get soft. Sauté garlic in a pan with some olive oil, then toss steamed beans in with the garlic oil, add soy sauce or tamari. Keep them crispy or cook until wrinkled; it's a taste preference. Salt to taste.

My kids like this recipe so much that we have certain days that are "all you can eat green bean night", when I make heaping bowls, enough to satisfy. Otherwise, they are portioned out for each person, but they always want more!

House in the Woods Farm
Adamstown, Maryland

Storage:

Fresh green beans taste best when eaten soon after harvesting. Store them in a plastic bag, with a damp paper towel, and they will stay fresh for up to one week in the refrigerator.

Cooking:

Just remove the stem end and then cook the beans whole. They will retain most of their nutrients if cooked uncut. You may cut them before cooking also. If you steam them with little water, or simmer them in more water, you can save the water to make soup stock! Cook only until the beans begin to brighten in color and become tender but not soft. You can cook them less, to keep them crispy, if you will be using them in chilled salads.

Favorite recipe:

3-5 cloves garlic, minced
Olive oil
1 lb. fresh green beans
1/4 cup tamari (gluten free)
1/2 cup chopped or slivered almonds

Sauté the garlic in the heated olive oil until they begin to just turn a bit brown around the edges, but be careful not to let them burn. Immediately add the green beans (you can add them whole or cut in half) and stir them continually until well coated with the oil and garlic. Stir frequently until they begin to brighten in color. Add the tamari, stir until all is well coated, cover and turn down the heat. Let the beans simmer for a few minutes, but don't over cook. Add the almonds, stir and serve with rice.

Winter Green Farm
Noti, Oregon

Herbs

Pesto can be made with almost anything green!

Freedom Farm
Houlton, Wisconsin

Wash, dry THOROUGHLY and chop all herbs together; store in an airtight container in the refrigerator and sprinkle on salads, sandwiches or into any dish! Also, use large pieces of basil, such as large lettuce-leaf basil, as a creative, tasty wrap!

Teena's Pride CSA
Homestead, Florida

IDEAS TO USE EVERY LAST LEAF OF HEAVENLY BASIL!

My favorite way to use basil is in a pesto to combine with pasta, to spread on a veggie sandwich, or to use as a dip, but it by no means ends there, that is just the beginning!

Here's a quick tip: tear several leaves of basil and place in a small bowl covered with extra virgin olive oil, sliced cherry tomatoes and sea salt. Marinade them for an entire day to heighten the flavor. Prepare your favorite pasta and pour entire contents of the bowl over warm, cooked pasta and stir gently. Sprinkle with sliced Kalamata olives if desired.

If you don't want to freeze pesto, then freeze basil mixed with a small amount of olive oil. Use in sauces. Another way to freeze basil is to place basil leaves in ice cube trays, cover with water and freeze. Pop into a zip lock bag and keep frozen until you need a hint of basil in a dish!

Kohlrabi

Kohlrabi is the alien-looking vegetable that is truly foreign to most CSA members (except those from Europe, where kohlrabi is more popular). In the spring on the first CSA pickup day that features kohlrabi, I give out samples to CSA members. I offer them peeled slices of raw kohlrabi! Just peel off the tough outer skin and slice. It's the best way to eat kohlrabi. It's great sliced or cut into strips like carrot sticks and then eaten with dip.

Kohlrabi tastes like the stem of broccoli. Kids tend to love it raw. My son likes to eat it peeled and whole, like an apple, right in the garden.

It's really best raw! But if I were going to cook kohlrabi, I'd lightly toss it in a stir-fry. It becomes mushy when overcooked.

House in the Woods Farm
Adamstown, Maryland

To make a simple kohlrabi slaw, wash and peel kohlrabi, then grate in the food processor. Also, grate carrots and onions or shallots, then toss in apple cider vinegar and olive oil to taste. Season with sea salt and freshly milled black pepper.

Honey Brook Organic Farm
Pennington, New Jersey

Leeks

Cleaning Leeks

Leeks grow by adding on layers, which allows dirt to settle in between and makes them tricky to clean. To facilitate cleaning, cut off the length of leek you plan to use (the white section plus any of the light green you want), then cut length-wise in half, cutting through the base. With the root end up holding your half leek together, fan the layers under running water, allowing the debris to run off into the sink.

Tecolote Farm-Oldest CSA in Texas
Austin, Texas

Parsnips

Parsnips will keep till spring in a plastic bag in the refrigerator. Peel thickly before use. Add to chicken soups with other vegetables. There's just something special that a couple of parsnips do to chicken soup!

Garden Patch Produce CSA
Alexandria, Ohio

Peel, chop, and add to a soup or stew.

Substitute a parsnip for a carrot in most recipes!

Roast them with other root vegetables.

Grate small parsnips into fresh salads.

Peppers

Peppers are one of our favorite things to grow; they come in so many shapes, sizes and colors. They can be prolific as well, but they are easy to freeze. They do not need blanching; simply freeze them for their future use, i.e. chopped. It's easier to remove the seeds prior to freezing. We like freezing them to be used for one of our favorite meals, stuffed peppers. Remove top; clean out seeds, to help pepper retain its shape stuff the cavity with crumpled wax paper, freezer paper, or plastic wrap. Place its top back on and freeze. Stuff while still frozen and bake.

Green Hill Farm
Shrewsbury, Massachusetts

Radishes

Radishes make great veggie chips! Slice them thinly and toss in a mixture of olive oil and sea salt (and any other desired seasonings), then bake at 275 F for 10 minutes, flip them to the other side and bake another 15 minutes. Check to make sure they are crispy but not overly browned.

Featherstone Farm
Rushford, Minnesota

If you're growing your own radishes, let a few of them bolt without harvesting them. After they flower, the seeds will start to develop inside green pods. Harvest the pods not long after they have formed, and you'll be rewarded with spicy little garden treats that are as crisp and fun to pop in your mouth as sugar snap peas!

Waltham Fields Community Farm
Community Farms Outreach, Inc.
Waltham, Massachusetts

Rutabaga

Simply peel off the outer skin and slice a rutabaga thinly. Dice or shred to add to salads, or grate to add to a veggie slaw. If you have other veggies such as a turnip, carrots, winter squash and leeks, then you are in luck! A simple root vegetable roast is a simple and versatile way to use a rutabaga. Mix with olive oil and sea salt and roast these veggies for about 45 minutes at 400 degrees F. Don't forget to add fresh herbs!

Salad Greens

Don't let your salads get boring! Wash salad leaves well in a salad spinner and dry well. Add any of these combinations of toppings or use what you have on hand!

1) Chopped carrots, celery, and Kalamata olives
2) Roasted sweet potatoes and raspberries
3) A scoop of hummus or guacamole
4) Tomato salsa, black beans, and avocado
5) Lentils, roasted peppers, and baby bella mushrooms
6) Sliced pear, dried cranberries, and almonds
7) Roasted beets and walnuts
8) Strawberries and hazelnuts
9) Roasted garlic, pickled eggplant and marinated mushrooms
10) Apples, roasted butternut squash, and caramelized onions

Sugar snap peas

Sugar Snap Peas should be eaten straight from the vine, in the garden, preferably with a dog. (Our dog loves snap peas.) Otherwise, lightly stir-fry in an Asian dish.

House in the Woods Farm
Adamstown, Maryland

Sweet Potato

Wash, scrub and pierce potatoes. Bake at 375 degrees F for about 45 minutes.

Sweet potato fries are a favorite with the kids at our house. Peel the potatoes if you wish, slice into thin, French-fry sized pieces. Mix together with some olive oil and kosher salt, then lay them in a baking pan/cookie sheet in the oven, 20 minutes at 350 degrees F will do it, but it really depends on how you slice the potatoes and how firm you like them.

Earth Dance Farm
Spring Valley, Minnesota

Tomatoes

Tomatoes are our specialty. We grow over 150 varieties each year and hold a big Tomato Festival with a tasting of tomatoes at our farm. The key that many people don't know about tomatoes is that they should not be refrigerated. The tropical fruit loses flavor when chilled and also can get chilling injury. Tomatoes should be stored at 55-60 degrees F or higher.

Oven Roasted Tomatoes

6 medium tomatoes, sliced crosswise, 1/2 to 3/4 inch thick
Olive oil
Salt, pepper and sugar

Heat oven to 300 degrees F. Line two baking sheets with aluminum foil; generously rub with oil. Arrange tomato slices in a single layer on prepared baking sheets. Sprinkle with salt, pepper and sugar. Roast until the tomatoes shrivel, the edges start to turn brown and most of the liquid around the tomatoes has caramelized, about 1 hour. Roasted tomatoes will keep 4 or 5 days in the refrigerator.

Red Fire Farm
Granby, Massachusetts

Chop and mix tomatoes, cucumbers and mint with onions, jalapenos and lime juice to create a quick, refreshing salsa.

Teena's Pride CSA
Homestead, Florida

Turnips

Add some extra vegetables to your dinner plate by including turnips in your mashed potatoes! Simply peel and boil your turnips, then puree them with your potatoes to add zing to this dinnertime classic. And don't forget those greens, either. Turnip greens can be boiled, stir-fried, or braised for a tasty, healthy side dish.

World Hunger Relief, Inc.
Waco, Texas

Slice turnips 1/4 inch thick, place 10 fresh sage leaves on turnips until their smell is released, set aside. Place turnips in a bit of hot oil (sunflower or olive oil) on medium high in a cast iron skillet until browned. Add salt and sage, continue to cook for two minutes. So delicious!

Rising Stone Farms
Portland, Oregon

Winter Squash

Roasted Winter Squash

Cut any type of winter squash into large chunks and mix with olive oil, maple syrup, and sea salt, just to coat. Transfer to a baking pan and roast at 400 degrees F until tender and caramelized. Enjoy as a winter side dish or add to chili and soups. Slice and add to Mexican foods like tacos or burritos. Use as a pizza topping. Use as a stuffing for ravioli or pierogies. Mix with warm apples and dried cranberries. Smash and add to waffle or pancake batter. There are so many uses for delicious, versatile winter squash!

Butternut squash "French fries." Halve, peel and cut your squash into French-fry size strips, place on a cookie sheet, brush with vegetable oil and bake in a regular oven at 375 degrees F for 15 minutes (or until done).

Fiddler's Greens, LLC
West Bloomfield, New York

Zucchini and Summer Squash

Zucchini and summer squash steal the show. Cook Once, Eat Twice!

How about grilling whatever veggies you have in abundance especially green and yellow squash, peppers, tomatoes, onions? Simply cut into bite-sized pieces and mix gently with olive oil and any herbs/spices of your choice, then grill. Meanwhile, make some tomato salsa, guacamole, and basil pesto. You are all set for two nights of meals!

Night One: Veggie Fajitas—with tomato salsa and guacamole!

Night Two: Pasta with basil pesto and grilled veggies!

Grate and freeze small batches of extra zucchini. Pop the zucchini in breads, cakes, soups and stews!

From The Simplest Garden Pantry comes an array of satisfying dishes

Apple cider vinegar
Balsamic vinegar
Chili powder
Cinnamon
Coconut milk
Corn meal
Dried beans/lentils
Extra virgin olive oil
Freshly ground pepper
Grainy brown mustard
Ground cumin
Hoisin Sauce (gluten free)
Hot pepper sauce
Kalamata olives
Maple syrup (local)
Nutmeg
Pecans
Pine Nuts
Rice (long grain basmati)
Sea salt
Tahini
Tamari (gluten free)
Unsweetened coconut flakes
Walnuts
White wine vinegar
Whole Oats (gluten free)

Basics

When you have these basics made and ready to use, cooking your vegetables becomes a joy!

Garden Vinaigrette

Keep this chilled and ready to sprinkle on just-picked veggies!

1 cup extra virgin olive oil
1/3 cup balsamic vinegar, white wine vinegar or lemon juice
1 teaspoon Dijon mustard
Handful of chopped herbs
A shake of sea salt

Mix well!

Or omit mustard and instead add 1 cup pureed strawberries and blend!

Vegetable Stock

If the recipe calls for veggie stock or broth, use this! Make batches ahead of time and freeze. Defrost to make quick soups and stews.

3 quarts cold water
2 celery stalks, chopped
2 carrots, peeled and chopped
2 medium onions, chopped
2 leeks, chopped
10 peppercorns
Sea salt
Sprigs of fresh herbs like thyme, oregano, and basil

Combine all ingredients in a large stockpot. Bring to boil. Reduce heat and simmer, uncovered for 45 minutes. Strain through sieve and discard solids. Let cool and refrigerate. Containers can be frozen for about three months.

Roasted Garlic

Squeeze into mashed potatoes; add to a green salad or use as a spread.

4 heads of garlic
4 tablespoons of olive oil
Sea salt and freshly ground pepper

Preheat oven to 400 degrees F. Slice off the top quarter inch of each garlic head. Place on tin foil. Brush olive oil and sprinkle salt and pepper on garlic heads. Wrap in tin foil and place in hot oven. Roast 35 minutes or until garlic is soft.

Roasted Peppers

Delicious on salads and sandwiches!

6 colorful peppers, halved and cleaned
6 cloves of garlic, minced
¼ cup olive oil
¼ cup balsamic vinegar
Handful of fresh basil
Sprig of fresh oregano
Sea salt and freshly ground pepper

Preheat oven to 425 degrees F. Place peppers in a bowl and mix with olive oil. Place on baking sheet and bake until black on edges. Cool and remove skin. Place them in a bowl and season with remaining ingredients. Add extra olive oil as needed.

Refrigerator Pickles

To create a spicier version of these pickles, add two thin slices of jalapeno pepper to the saucepan before boiling.

6 cups sliced cucumbers
2 cups thinly sliced onions
1 1/4 cup apple cider vinegar
3/4 cup Florida crystals (or sweetener of your choice)
3/4 teaspoon sea salt
1/2 teaspoon mustard seeds
1/2 teaspoon celery seeds
1/2 teaspoon ground turmeric
1/4 teaspoon freshly ground pepper
4 garlic cloves, thinly sliced

Place three cups cucumber in a medium glass bowl; top with one cup of onion. Repeat with remaining three cups cucumber and remaining one cup of onion. Combine vinegar and remaining ingredients in a small saucepan; stir well. Bring to a boil; cook 1 minute. Pour over cucumber mixture, let cool. Cover and chill at least four days. Pickles may be stored in fridge for up to one month.

Basic Tomato Salsa

3 ripe tomatoes peeled, seeded and chopped
2 small cucumbers, sliced, seeds removed, and chopped
½ cup red onion, minced
¼ jalapeno pepper, seeded and minced
2 tablespoons fresh lime juice
A pinch of sea salt

Stir ingredients gently and refrigerate.

Preserved Lemons

I received this recipe several years ago from Be Wise Ranch CSA in San Diego, California. These lemons add a delicious flavor to so many dishes! Add to pesto, stews, lentil dishes, and vinaigrettes!

Whole Meyer lemons, preferably organic
More lemons for juicing
Sea salt
Glass jar with non-metal, tight sealing lid

Add one to two tablespoons of salt into the bottom of the jar. Cut lemons, but don't completely separate into quarters. Generously salt insides of lemons, and process into jar. (It's okay if they separate.) Compress all cut and salted lemons into a jar so that no space is left. Add fresh lemon juice to cover lemons. Add two more tablespoons of salt. Cover. Shake this beautifully brilliant jar daily. Let it sit as a decorative piece on your counter. Mark your calendar for 6 weeks, and then enjoy for up to one year refrigerated.

Pesto, Salsa, Dips and Sauces

Roasted Garlic and Herb Spread

A quick, delicious spread, right from your herb garden!

4 heads of garlic, roasted
3 tablespoons extra virgin olive oil
A mixture of fresh herbs like basil, rosemary, parsley, thyme, oregano, chopped
Sea salt and freshly ground pepper

In a bowl, mix roasted garlic with olive oil and chopped herbs until mixture comes together as a thick paste. Add sea salt and pepper. Use as a spread.

White Bean and Garlic Scape Dip

1/3 cup sliced garlic scapes (3 to 4)
1 tablespoon freshly squeezed lemon juice, more to taste
1/2 teaspoon coarse sea salt, more to taste
Freshly ground pepper, to taste
2 cups cannellini beans, cooked
1/4 cup extra virgin olive oil, more for drizzling.

In a food processor or blender, process garlic scapes with lemon juice, salt and pepper until finely chopped. Add cannellini beans and process to a rough purée. Add olive oil and a bit of water until you reach desired consistency. Add extra salt and pepper, if desired, and drizzle with olive oil.

Hummus

This classic pairs well with all types of vegetables.

2 cup dried garbanzo beans (chickpeas)
¾ cup tahini
6 tablespoons of extra virgin olive oil
10 cloves of garlic, minced
Juice of 3-4 lemons
½ teaspoon of ground cumin
Sea salt

Rinse and soak beans for two to three hours. Drain beans and bring to slow boil for one hour or until soft. Drain beans and combine all ingredients in a food processor and process until soft. Add water if mixture is too thick. Add lemon juice and sea salt to taste.

Fresh Pea Hummus

A light and fresh dip. Don't stop at peas, add some fresh herbs to your hummus for some zing.

2 cups fresh, shelled peas
1 cup cannellini beans, cooked
4 tablespoons tahini
4 tablespoons lemon juice
2 cloves of garlic
1/4 teaspoon cumin
Sea salt

Bring a small pot of water to a boil. Add peas and cook until tender, about 2 minutes. Drain and run under cold water. In a food processor or blender pulse peas, beans, tahini, lemon juice, garlic, cumin and salt.

Basil Pesto

Feel free to make this traditional pesto in large batches, because it freezes well for up to 3 months or refrigerate for up to 5 days!

¼ cup pine nuts
2 garlic cloves, peeled
¼ cup extra virgin olive oil
¼ cup veggie broth
4 cups basil leaves

Process ingredients in a food processor or blend in a blender until finely minced.

Garlic Scape Pesto

I choose walnuts when making pesto. They are rich in Omegas and add the perfect nutty taste to a pesto. To further heighten the flavors, use walnut oil instead of olive oil.

1 cup of garlic scapes, chopped, flowery parts removed
1 cup of flat leaf parsley
½ cup walnuts
2 tablespoons of extra virgin olive oil
½ cup of vegetable broth

Puree all ingredients in food processor or blender until smooth.

Cilantro Pesto

Cilantro may help eliminate mercury from our bodies.

4 cups of cilantro
½ cup pine nuts
2 tablespoons of extra virgin olive oil
1 shallot, chopped
½ cup of vegetable broth

Puree all ingredients in food processor or blender until smooth.

Marinara

2 tablespoons olive oil
5 garlic cloves, minced or pressed
1 tablespoon dried parsley
12 Roma tomatoes, halved lengthwise, quickly blended
1 teaspoon red pepper flakes
Sea salt
A handful of fresh basil, chopped

Heat oil in a medium saucepan over medium heat. Add garlic; sauté until light golden. Then add parsley. Stir one minute and add blended tomatoes, red pepper and salt. Simmer for about 20 minutes stirring occasionally. Add basil and cook five minutes more.

Note: Seeds may be removed from this sauce after cooking. Simply push the tomato sauce through a sieve into a bowl. Discard seeds.

Puttanesca Sauce: For a simple version of this spicy sauce use the marinara recipe. However, double the amount of garlic, add crushed red pepper to your liking, and stir in about 20 sliced Kalamata olives.

Mushroom sauce: With a tablespoon of extra virgin olive oil in the pan, sauté about 20 sliced baby bella mushrooms until almost soft. Drain and add to cooked marinara sauce.

Veggie Tomato Sauce

This sauce is also a slow cooker dinner!

1 large onion, chopped
1 large carrot, chopped
4 celery stalks, chopped
2 tablespoons rosemary
4 garlic cloves, minced
2 cups of sliced baby bellas
4 cups veggie broth
3 cups tomatoes, peeled, diced and blended
1 cup red wine
20 sliced Kalamata olives
A handful of basil, chopped
Freshly ground pepper

In a large saucepan sauté onions, carrots, and celery for five minutes. Add rosemary and garlic for one minute. Add mushrooms and continue to sauté over medium heat until soft. Add broth, tomatoes and wine. Simmer for 30 minutes to 2 hours. (If using slow cooker cook for 4 hours on high or 7 hours on low.) Add more tomatoes if needed. Add olives and basil 10 minutes before sauce has reached desired consistency. Season with black pepper.

Late Summer Garden Sauce

Try this no-cook tomato sauce on a hot day!

4 ripe tomatoes, peeled and quartered
1 handful of flat leaf parsley leaves, washed
1 handful of basil leaves, washed
½ cup extra virgin olive oil
Sea salt and freshly ground pepper

Combine all ingredients in a blender and blend until creamy. Serve with pasta.

Make-It-Your-Own Salsa

Chop any amount of any of these ingredients and also add anything else that you can imagine in a salsa. Have fun and let your CSA or garden dictate what type of salsa you'll be dipping into tonight!

2 cups chopped plum tomatoes
1 cup chopped cucumber
1 cup fresh corn kernels
1 cup black beans
1 cup chopped avocado
1 cup chopped red bell pepper
¼ cup chopped green onion
¼ cup chopped red onion
2 tablespoons of cilantro or flat leaf parsley, chopped
3 tablespoons fresh lime juice
1 tablespoon jalapeno pepper, chopped and seeded
1 tablespoon balsamic vinegar
Sea salt
Freshly ground pepper

Combine and stir well.

Tropical Salsa

2 cups chopped fresh mango
2 cups diced pineapple
⅓ cup chopped green onions
¼ cup minced seeded jalapeno
½ cup diced red bell pepper
⅓ cup fresh lime juice
Sea salt

Combine all ingredients and mix well. Serve immediately or refrigerate.

Yellow Tomato Salsa

2 yellow medium-sized Brandywine heirloom tomatoes, seeded and diced
2 cloves of garlic, minced
1 yellow pepper, chopped
½ of a medium cucumber, chopped
½ cup of chopped cilantro
1 small jalapeno chili, minced
3 tablespoons of fresh lime juice
Sea salt to taste

Combine all ingredients and then sprinkle with salt. Let sit for 30 minutes.

Guacamole

Guacamole gradually darkens when exposed to air so serve immediately. To lessen guacamole's color change, add lime juice, and stir well. Also try hot pepper sauce instead of the chili pepper.

4 ripe avocados
2 tablespoons finely chopped onion
2 fresh Serrano chili peppers, seeded and finely chopped
Fresh lime juice
Sea salt

Cut avocados in half, remove pits, and squeeze or scoop pulp into a bowl. Mash with fork. Add onions and peppers. Mix well with fork. Season to taste with salt and lime juice.

Roasted Eggplant and Garlic Caviar

1 large eggplant
4 large garlic cloves
3 tablespoons lemon juice
2 scallions, chopped
1 small handful of flat leaf parsley
3 tablespoons olive oil
Sea salt

Preheat oven to 400 degrees F. Pierce eggplant about five times with a fork and place it on a baking sheet. Pour a slight amount of water on baking sheet and place in oven. Place garlic cloves in wrapped tin foil and place in oven. Turn eggplant once and roast eggplant and garlic for about 40 minutes.

Remove from heat and cool. Once eggplant is cool, slice it in half removing and spooning the flesh into a blender. Squeeze the garlic out of its skin and into the blender also. Add remaining ingredients and season with sea salt. Serve at room temperature. The caviar can be refrigerated for several days, and it freezes well.

Salads

Grilled Asparagus Salad

Asparagus and Kalamata olives are a perfect pairing. Love asparagus on the grill? Take it to the next level with this summer salad.

Salad:

1 head of Boston lettuce, leaves washed and separated
1-1/2 pounds of asparagus
10 Kalamata olives, sliced

Vinaigrette:

¼ cup extra virgin olive oil
4 tablespoons of balsamic vinegar
1 teaspoon of Dijon mustard
Sea salt and freshly ground pepper

Preheat gas grill or broiler. Place lettuce leaves on a platter. Combine all vinaigrette ingredients. Brush asparagus with vinaigrette and grill until tender for about 8 minutes. Place asparagus over lettuce, and then top with olives.

Beet, Turnip and Radish Salad

1 red onion, thinly sliced
2 garlic cloves, crushed
1 small bell pepper, cored, seeded and thinly sliced
¼ cup extra virgin olive oil
¼ cup white wine vinegar
Sea salt and freshly ground pepper
3 tablespoons fresh thyme
4 handfuls of lettuce leaves, washed
5 medium beets, scrubbed, boiled, peeled and cooled
3 small salad/spring turnips, thinly sliced
5 small radishes, thinly sliced

Place onion, garlic, bell pepper, olive oil, vinegar, salt, black pepper and thyme in a bowl. Toss and marinade for an hour. Meanwhile, place lettuce in a salad bowl. Top with beets, turnips and radishes. Pour marinade over salad and toss gently.

Broccoli Salad

7 cups of broccoli florets
4 garlic cloves, minced
20 pitted Kalamata olives, sliced
¼ cups lemon juice
1/2 cup extra virgin olive oil
Sea salt and freshly ground pepper

Steam broccoli until tender and crisp. Immediately immerse into iced water and drain. Place broccoli on a platter, sprinkle with garlic, olives, lemon juice, and olive oil. Stir gently. Add salt and pepper to taste. Serve at room temperature.

Asian Slaw

1 small piece of ginger, grated finely
¾ cup white wine vinegar
Juice of one lime
1 tablespoon tamari
¼ cup sesame oil

Combine above ingredients and set aside.

1 head cabbage, sliced thin
2 bell peppers, sliced thin
1 jalapeno, finely minced
4 scallions, white and light green parts chopped
1 small handful of fresh mint, chopped
1 cup sliced toasted almonds

Combine all ingredients in a large salad bowl. Gently toss with vinaigrette. Flavors heightened while chilled.

Black Bean and Corn Salad

4 cups black beans, cooked
4 ears of corn, steamed and kernels removed
1 red pepper, chopped
1 small red onion, chopped
1 avocado, sliced
3 tablespoons of extra virgin olive oil
¼ cup white wine vinegar
The zest and juice of one lime

Combine all ingredients in a salad bowl and toss gently.

Sizzling Eggplant Salad

Fresh salsa is delicious mixed in any salad, but it is especially delicious when paired with grilled eggplant. This is a great salad when it's too hot to light the oven!

Olive oil
2 large eggplants, peeled and sliced 1/2 inch thick
2 cups fresh salsa
2 cups black beans, cooked
2 tablespoons lime juice
Sea salt and freshly ground pepper

Preheat gas grill or prepare charcoal fire. Brush oil onto one side of eggplant slices, place on grill, oiled side down. Cook 6 to 8 minutes until tender. Brush oil on tops and turn and grill until tender another 6 to 8 minutes. Cool slightly and then chop on cutting board. Combine eggplant, fresh salsa, black beans and lime juice in a large salad bowl; toss to mix. Add salt and pepper as needed.

Marinated Cucumber Salad

This recipe creates delicate, slightly pickled cucumbers. Delicious!

4 medium cucumbers, thinly sliced
1 cup thinly sliced onion
2 garlic cloves, thinly sliced
½ cup maple syrup
1 cup apple cider vinegar
4 tablespoons chopped fresh dill
Freshly ground pepper

Place cucumbers and onion in a bowl. Combine garlic, syrup, and vinegar in a small saucepan. Bring to a boil, cook one minute, stirring. Pour over cucumber mixture and marinade for two hours, stirring occasionally. Drain cucumbers and sprinkle with dill and pepper to taste. Mix well and chill.

Summer Cucumber Salad

2 cups chickpeas, cooked
2 cucumbers, halved and sliced thinly
1 cup Kalamata olives, pitted and sliced
2 green onions, chopped
A handful of flat-leaf parsley, washed and chopped
¼ cup extra virgin olive oil
¼ cup balsamic vinegar
1 tablespoon grainy mustard
Sea salt and freshly ground pepper

Combine chickpeas, cucumbers, olives, onions, and parsley in a serving bowl. In a small mixing bowl whisk olive oil, vinegar, mustard, salt and pepper. Pour vinaigrette over the cucumber salad and toss gently. Chill until ready to serve.

Nicoise Salad

8 cups of green beans, cleaned with stems removed
8 small red potatoes, quartered
4 garlic cloves, minced
1 cup of sliced Kalamata olives
Handful of fresh herbs like flat-leaf parsley, basil, oregano, mint
1 cup white wine vinegar
½ cup extra virgin olive oil

Steam beans for five minutes in a medium saucepan and then immerse in cold water to stop the cooking process. Drain. Gently boil potatoes until soft. Drain. Combine all ingredients in a salad bowl and mix.

Strawberry Salad

4 cups arugula
1 pint of strawberries, cleaned and sliced
4 scallions, cleaned and white and light green parts sliced
3 tablespoons extra virgin olive oil
¼ cup white wine vinegar
2 tablespoons of maple syrup
1 cup sliced toasted almonds

Combine arugula, strawberries and scallions in a salad bowl. Combine oil, vinegar and syrup in a small bowl. Pour mixture over salad and toss. Sprinkle with toasted almonds.

Orange and Arugula Salad

2 large handfuls of baby arugula, cleaned
½ medium red onion, sliced
½ cup Kalamata olives, pitted
1 juicy orange, peeled and sliced
½ cup white wine vinegar
¼ cup extra virgin olive oil
Sea salt and freshly ground pepper, to taste

Place all ingredients in the bowl and toss gently.

Spring Salad

Make this salad with veggies straight from your garden and notice as you slowly take each bite just how miraculous vegetables are! It is incredible how little we really need to "dress up" farm-fresh veggies.

2 heads of butterhead, Boston or bibb lettuce, washed
4 radishes, trimmed and sliced thinly
1 large carrot, peeled and cut into thin strips
4 tablespoons of white wine vinegar
6 tablespoons extra virgin olive oil
Sea salt and freshly ground pepper

Tear lettuce into small pieces. Add lettuce, radishes and carrots to a bowl. Whisk vinegar, oil, and salt and pepper and pour over salad. Toss gently.

Edamame Chopped Salad

Salad:
2 cups frozen shelled edamame
4 cups chopped lettuce
1 cup scallions, chopped
1 cup Kalamata olives, sliced
2 cups cucumber, chopped
1 red pepper, cored, cleaned and chopped
½ cup fresh Italian parsley

Dressing:
2/3 cup extra virgin olive oil
1/3 cup orange, lime or lemon juice
5 garlic cloves, minced
Sea salt and freshly ground pepper

Cook edamame in a pan of water on medium heat for about five minutes. Drain and cool. Make dressing by combining all ingredients and mix well. Place all salad ingredients in a large bowl. Sprinkle with edamame and drizzle dressing over salad. Toss lightly and serve.

Guacamole Salad

Serve chilled as a dip, condiment or a side salad. Delicious spread on a grilled veggie sandwich!

4 avocados, peeled, pitted and chopped
2 ears of corn, steamed and kernels removed
1 cucumber, peeled and chopped
10 cherry tomatoes, chopped
1 cup chopped red onion
The juice of one lime
2 garlic cloves, minced
2 tablespoons hot pepper sauce

Gently toss ingredients together.

Tomato salad

3 large juicy tomatoes, chopped
2 cold cucumbers, sliced
4 garlic cloves, minced
10 Kalamata olives, sliced
½ cup chopped red onion
1 cup of chick peas, cooked
¼ cup extra virgin olive oil
¼ cup balsamic vinegar
1 tablespoon fresh oregano, chopped
Sea salt and freshly ground pepper

Combine all ingredients in a chilled bowl. Stir carefully.

Tomato and Peach Salad

4 large tomatoes
3 large ripe but still firm peaches, peeled and cut into wedges
2 teaspoons of fresh tarragon leaves or other favorite herb
1/2 cup summer vinaigrette

Lay out the tomatoes and peaches on serving platter and sprinkle tarragon leaves over top.
Pour vinaigrette over all and chill for at least one hour, then serve.

Summer Vinaigrette

4 tablespoons white wine vinegar
¼ cup light olive oil
Pinch sea salt
Pinch of white pepper

Spring Roll Salad

Pac choi is also known as bok choy and Chinese cabbage and has many spelling variations. Pac choi is related to the cabbage family and belongs to the same vegetable species as the turnip.

1 pack thin rice noodles – cook and save some of the water
2 small bunches of Pac Choi thinly sliced including the greens
1 bunch green onions, thinly sliced including some of the green
1 cup diced cucumber
1 grated carrot
Handful of chopped mint
Handful of chopped cilantro

Toss together.

Make a dressing using:

½ cup of the reserved water
½ cup chunky peanut butter
¼ cup Hoisin sauce (or less depending on your taste)
A dash of hot sauce

If serving later, wait to add the dressing. Add other veggies and make this salad your own!

Warm Potato Salad

Quick side dish for a barbecue!

3 lbs. Yukon gold potatoes, scrubbed and quartered
8 scallions, chopped
2 cloves of garlic, minced
¾ cup fresh parsley, chopped
1/3 cup white wine vinegar
¼ cup extra virgin olive oil
Sea salt and freshly ground pepper to taste

Gently boil potatoes until soft. Drain and transfer potatoes into a bowl. Add remaining ingredients and stir. Serve warm.

Radish and Spring Turnip Salad

12 small radishes, thinly sliced
3 small salad/spring turnips, thinly sliced
1 teaspoon toasted sesame oil
2 teaspoons white wine vinegar
Juice of 1 lime
1 tablespoon chopped chives
Sea salt, to taste

Combine all ingredients in a bowl. Stir gently but thoroughly to combine and coat all the slices. Season with sea salt.

Sweet Potato Salad

Great side dish for Thanksgiving!

3 lbs. sweet potatoes, peeled, cut into 2 inch pieces
¼ cup maple syrup
¼ cup grainy, brown mustard
1 cup pecans (can be toasted)
1 cup dried cranberries

Gently boil potatoes until soft. Drain potatoes and transfer potatoes into a bowl. Mix maple syrup and mustard and pour over potatoes. Sprinkle pecans and cranberries on salad and gently stir.

Citrus-Infused Zucchini Salad

When you need to serve a new and different dish at a picnic, and when your supply of zucchini is at its maximum, this salad is the perfect choice!

Salad:

3 cups julienne-cut zucchini
1-1/2 cups fresh corn kernels (about 3 ears)
10 Kalamata olives, sliced
3 tablespoons of finely chopped chives
3 tablespoons of finely chopped basil

Toss all salad ingredients in a bowl.

Citrus vinaigrette:

4 tablespoons of fresh orange juice
2 tablespoons of fresh lime juice
2 teaspoons of maple syrup
2 tablespoons of extra virgin olive oil
1 teaspoon of white wine vinegar
Sea salt and freshly ground pepper

Combine all vinaigrette ingredients and blend. Add vinaigrette to salad and toss well. Chill until ready to serve.

Soups and Stews

Mediterranean Stew

Take full advantage of fresh herbs! They add life energy to our dishes like nothing else!

1 onion, sliced
6 garlic cloves, pressed
6 large portabella mushrooms, sliced
5 colorful bell peppers, seeded and sliced
1 large zucchini, sliced
3 ripe medium tomatoes, chopped
1/2 cup red wine
3 cups of chick peas, cooked
2 cups of pitted Kalamata olives
5 tablespoons of a mixture of chopped fresh rosemary, thyme, oregano
Sea salt and freshly ground pepper

Put the onion, garlic, mushrooms, peppers and zucchini in a large sauce pan over medium heat. Add tomatoes, red wine, and chick peas, mixing well. Cover and simmer for about 30 minutes until the vegetables are tender crisp. Remove lid and cook on medium high, stirring occasionally. Stir in olives and herbs. Serve immediately.

Kale and White Bean Soup

2 tablespoons extra virgin olive oil
2 celery stalks, chopped
2 carrots, peeled and chopped
1 large onion, chopped
6 cloves of garlic, minced or pressed
2 rosemary sprigs, leaves removed from sprig
2 thyme sprigs, leaves removed from sprig
1-1/2 lbs. of red potatoes, washed and cut into small pieces
8 cups of veggie broth
4 cups of cooked cannellini beans
2 cups of kale, washed and chopped
Freshly ground pepper

Sauté celery, carrots and onion in olive oil until soft. Add garlic, rosemary and thyme and sauté for one more minute. Add red potatoes and veggie broth. Simmer on medium heat until potatoes are soft, about 20 minutes. Add beans, kale and ground pepper. Soup is ready when kale is bright green and tender.

Southern Veggie Soup

Easy slow cooker meal too!

1 tablespoon of olive oil
1 medium onion, chopped
2 celery stalks, cleaned and chopped
2 medium carrots, peeled and chopped
6 cups veggie broth
2 cups potatoes, diced
5 large tomatoes, chopped well or blended
1 teaspoon dried basil
1 teaspoon dried thyme
2 cups lima beans, cooked
2 cups okra, cleaned and sliced
4 ears of corn, shucked and kernels removed
Sea salt and freshly ground pepper

Place oil at the bottom of a large soup pot. Add onions, celery and carrots and sauté for about 5 minutes on medium heat. Add broth, potatoes, tomatoes, basil and thyme. Cover and simmer for 30 minutes. Add lima beans, okra, and corn. Cook 15 minutes longer. Season with sea salt and pepper to taste.

Lentils and Greens Soup

3 tablespoons olive oil
1 large onion, chopped
2 celery stalks, chopped
2 carrots, peeled and chopped
2 teaspoons ground cumin
4 cloves of garlic, pressed
1 tablespoon fresh oregano
2 cup lentils
5-6 cup of vegetable broth
2 cups of greens (baby spinach, kale, chard)
Sea salt and freshly ground pepper, to taste

In a large pot over medium heat, add olive oil, onion, celery and carrots. Sauté until onion is translucent. Add cumin, garlic, and oregano and stir for one minute. Immediately add lentils and broth. Reduce heat, cover and simmer until lentils are soft. Season with sea salt and pepper to taste.

Meanwhile, clean greens well. Chop kale or chard into small pieces if using. Mix greens well into soup and cover for about 7 minutes; baby spinach will take a shorter amount of time to wilt in soup. Serve immediately.

Sweet Potato Chowder

1 tablespoon olive oil
1 onion, chopped
3 garlic cloves, minced
4 ears fresh corn
5 medium sweet potatoes, peeled and chopped
1/3 cup yellow corn meal
5 cups veggie broth
1 tablespoon maple syrup
1 teaspoon ground cinnamon
¼ teaspoon nutmeg
Sea salt and freshly ground pepper

Heat oil in a large pot; add onion and sauté. When onion is soft, add garlic and sauté for two minutes. Scrape kernels off of corn and add in pot stirring quickly. Then add sweet potatoes, corn meal, and broth. Bring to boil over medium heat, then lower heat and cover. Simmer until potatoes become soft. Puree soup in a blender or with an immersion blender. Return to stove and stir in maple syrup, cinnamon and nutmeg. Season with salt and pepper.

Light Spring Soup

This soup screams SPRING! Many times after preparing this soup, I sit quietly and decide just what seeds I'd like to plant in my own life. From new projects that fall outside of my comfort zone to old hobbies that I'd like to reclaim, the spring is the best time to start creating!

3 tablespoons olive oil
1 large onion, diced
4 cloves of garlic, minced
4 cups veggie broth
2 small zucchini, cut into ½ inch chunks
1 cup thinly sliced baby bella mushrooms
2 cups sliced asparagus
2 cups baby spinach
2 cups baby peas
2 cups cannellini beans, cooked
½ cup fresh flat leaf parsley
Sea salt and freshly ground pepper, to taste

Heat olive oil in a large pot. Add onions, sauté about 7 minutes. Add garlic and sauté about 1 minute. Add broth, zucchini, mushrooms, and asparagus, cook 5 minutes. Add spinach, peas and beans and cook 5 minutes more on low heat. Stir in parsley, salt and pepper.

"Creamy" Asparagus Soup

3 pounds asparagus
4 tablespoons extra virgin olive oil
4 cups onion, chopped
1 cup uncooked basmati rice
12 cups vegetable broth
2 tablespoons of chopped thyme
2 tablespoons of chopped rosemary
Freshly ground pepper

Use all asparagus except ends. Trim tips and reserve. Cut remaining asparagus into small pieces. Add olive oil and onion to a large stockpot. Sauté onions until soft. Add remaining ingredients, cover and simmer for about 25 minutes. When rice becomes soft, transfer batches of soup into a blender or use immersion blender. Blend until creamy. Return soup to pot and add asparagus tips. Simmer for three minutes until tips are bright green and serve immediately.

"Creamy" Garlic Soup

2 tablespoons extra virgin olive oil
1 large onion, chopped
12 cloves of garlic, minced or pressed
2 rosemary sprigs, leaves removed from sprig
2 thyme sprigs, leaves removed from sprig
6 cups of veggie broth
4 cups of cooked cannellini beans
Freshly ground black pepper

In a large pot, sauté onion in olive oil until soft, add garlic, rosemary and thyme and sauté for one more minute. Add veggie broth and beans. Simmer on medium heat for about 20 minutes. Transfer batches of soup into a blender or use immersion blender. Blend until creamy. Return soup to pot, add ground pepper and serve.

Gazpacho

5 ripe tomatoes, blended
¼ cup onion, minced
2 cloves garlic, minced
1 medium cucumber, minced
1 bell pepper, minced
½ teaspoon cumin
Juice of one lime
A handful of fresh flat-leaf parsley, minced
Sea salt and freshly ground pepper

Combine any or all of these ingredients using your senses to determine amounts! Mince ingredients or quickly blend all in a blender or food processor. Chill.

Roasted Heirloom Tomato Bisque

2-3 pounds of heirloom tomatoes
1 head of medium garlic, peeled
¼ cup olive oil
1 teaspoon fresh thyme leaves, chopped
3 cups veggie broth
1 cup almond milk or unsweetened coconut milk beverage

Heat oven to 400 degrees F. In a large mixing bowl combine tomatoes, garlic, olive oil and thyme. Spread onto a large baking sheet and roast for about 30 minutes, stirring once. Add roasted tomatoes and broth into a large soup pot. Cook for about 15 minutes. Blend with immersion blender or transfer portions of the soup into a blender, blending all of the soup. Return soup to pot and add milk. Stir well and serve.

Winter Squash—Lentil Soup

1 tablespoon extra virgin olive oil
1 carrot, peeled and chopped
1 celery stalk, peeled and chopped
1 large onion, chopped
1 large butternut squash or equivalent, peeled, seeded and cut into chunks
1 teaspoon of dried rosemary
1 teaspoon of dried thyme
5 cups veggie broth
1 cup lentils, rinsed
Sea salt and freshly ground pepper

Heat oil in a large pot. Add carrot, celery and onion and sauté until soft, about 10 minutes. Add the squash, rosemary and thyme and combine. Add veggie broth and simmer covered for about 20 minutes or until butternut squash is fork tender. Meanwhile in a medium saucepan add lentils, cover with water and simmer until lentils are soft, about 20 to 25 minutes. Drain. Use blender or immersion blender and puree soup mixture. Once pureed, stir in lentils and season.

Apple-Butternut Bisque

Crock-pot friendly!

1 butternut squash, peeled, cleaned and diced
1 onion, chopped
2 cloves of garlic, halved
2 Granny Smith apples, peeled, cored and sliced
3 Macintosh apples, peeled, cored and sliced
6 cups of veggie broth
1-1/2 tablespoons of cinnamon
1 teaspoon nutmeg
1 tablespoon of chili powder
1 cup unsweetened coconut milk beverage

Combine all ingredients in a large pot. Cover and simmer for 30 minutes or until butternut squash is tender. Remove batches of the soup and blend until all soup is completely blended or use an immersion blender. Stir in milk.

Garden Chili

Pumpkin makes a surprise appearance in this farm fresh chili. Stir in some brown rice or quinoa for a heartier meal. Pour over tortilla chips for a fun appetizer.

2 bell peppers, chopped
1 onion, chopped
1 tablespoon extra virgin olive oil
3 tablespoons chili powder
2 tablespoons ground cumin
3 garlic cloves, pressed
5 to 6 tomatoes, blended
4 cups water
2 small zucchini, chopped
3 ears of corn, kernels removed
2 cups cooked and mashed pumpkin
2 cups red kidney beans, cooked
2 cups black beans, cooked

Sauté peppers and onions with olive oil for about five minutes. Add chili powder, cumin and garlic until fragrant, about one minute. Add blended tomatoes, water, zucchini, and pumpkin. Simmer on medium-low for 20 minutes. Add beans and corn until hot. Serve or store.

Main Dishes

Butternut Squash Chili over Corn Spaghetti

1 butternut squash, peeled, cleaned, diced
2 tablespoons olive oil
2 onions, chopped
2 bell peppers, chopped
4 cloves of garlic, minced
1/4 cup chili powder
1-2 teaspoons cinnamon
5 to 6 whole tomatoes, blended
4 cups red kidney beans
8 oz. corn spaghetti

Preheat oven to 400 degrees F and roast butternut squash with 1 tablespoon of olive oil in a deep roasting pan for 30 minutes. Place the other tablespoon of olive oil in a large saucepan and sauté on medium heat with onion and peppers until veggies are soft. Add garlic and stir for one minute. Add chili power, cinnamon and tomato. Simmer gently for 20 minutes stirring occasionally. Add beans and roasted squash and stir to mix flavors together. Serve over corn spaghetti.

Ratatouille—Two Ways

Whether you simmer your luscious veggies in a slow cooker or for a twist, grill them outdoors. When you make ratatouille, it's summer!

When you plan an afternoon in the garden, yet long to come inside for a hot meal, ratatouille is a perfect choice. Create your perfect mixture of veggies based on what you harvested that week.

¼ cup olive oil
2 cup cubed, peeled eggplant
1 cup chopped zucchini
1/2 cup chopped tomatoes
1 red or yellow pepper, chopped
1 red onion, chopped
4 cloves garlic, chopped
2 teaspoons thyme
2 teaspoons oregano
½ cup veggie broth
Sea salt and freshly ground pepper, to taste
2 tablespoons fresh basil

Sauté eggplant, zucchini, tomatoes, pepper, and onion in olive oil until soft. Stir in remaining ingredients except basil. Transfer vegetable mixture to a slow cooker and cook on low heat for 4-1/2 hours or on high-heat setting for 2-1/2 hours, or simmer for an additional 25 minutes. Stir basil into mixture when ready to serve. Freezes well!

Grilled Ratatouille

1/3 cup extra virgin olive oil
3 tablespoons of lemon juice
1 yellow pepper, stemmed, seeded and halved
1 red pepper, stemmed, seeded and halved
2 Vidalia onions, peeled and sliced in rounds
1 large zucchini, sliced into ¼ inch slices
1 small eggplant unpeeled, sliced into 1/4 inch rounds
2 dozen cherry tomatoes, sliced in half
2 tablespoons of balsamic vinegar
½ cup fresh basil, chopped
1 tablespoon fresh oregano
Sea salt and freshly ground pepper

Preheat grill to medium-high. Place olive oil, lemon juice, peppers, onions, zucchini and eggplant in a large bowl. Gently turn to coat veggies. Grill veggies until tender, turning once. Cool slightly and chop grilled veggies into bite-size pieces. Toss in a large bowl with remaining ingredients. Serve warm.

Veggie Shepard's Pie

Turn roasted veggies into a delicious main meal!

Roast some veggies in either summer or winter and create a delicious Shepard's pie!

Start with about 5 sweet potatoes, peeled, cut, cooked, and mashed. Add some coconut milk beverage and olive oil and stir well. Place roasted veggies at the bottom of a shallow baking dish, sprinkle with peas or beans and top with mashed sweet potatoes. Bake until warm throughout.

Roasted Veggies with Fresh Herbs

2 cups zucchini, halved and cut into 1 inch chunks
12 oz. baby bella mushrooms, trimmed
2 cups cauliflower florets
2 cups baby carrots
1 yellow onion, chopped
2 cloves of garlic, minced
1/3 cup olive oil
2 tablespoons chopped fresh oregano
2 tablespoons chopped fresh thyme
2 tablespoons chopped fresh rosemary
1 teaspoon sea salt
½ teaspoon freshly ground pepper

Preheat oven to 425 degrees F. Toss all ingredients in a large bowl. Transfer vegetables to baking sheet or roasting pan. Roast 30 minutes or until all vegetables are brown and tender. Turn vegetables periodically. Transfer vegetables back to large bowl and serve.

Roasted Winter Veggies

Olive oil
3 sweet potatoes, peeled and cut into cubes
3 cups winter squash, peeled, seeded and cut into cubes
2 turnips, peeled and cut into cubes
3 parsnips, halved lengthwise and cut into short pieces
4 carrots, halved lengthwise and cut into pieces
3 garlic cloves, chopped
3 tablespoons olive oil
1 tablespoon dried thyme
1 tablespoon dried rosemary

Preheat oven to 400 degrees F. Coat a roasting pan with olive oil. Place all ingredients in a roasting pan and stir gently. Roast for 20 minutes, stir, and continue to roast for an additional 20 minutes or until veggies are fork tender. Serve immediately.

Butternut Green Risotto

About 3-1/2 cups veggie broth
2 tablespoons of extra virgin olive oil
1 onion, chopped
3 cloves of garlic, minced
1 teaspoon dried rosemary
1 teaspoon dried thyme
1-1/2 cups diced butternut squash
1 cup Arborio rice
4 tablespoons dry white wine or mirin
1 cup or more greens such as kale, chard or spinach, chopped
Sea salt and freshly ground pepper

Warm the broth and reserve. In a medium saucepan heat olive oil, place onions in pan and sauté until tender. Add garlic, rosemary and thyme and cook for two minutes. Add squash, rice and wine. Add enough broth to cover rice. Add more broth each time broth has been absorbed. When most but not all of the broth is absorbed, add greens and season. Stir often until rice has a "creamy" consistency, about 20 minutes.

Baked Winter Squash Risotto

When many dishes are being prepared on the stove-top, it's nice to pull a baked risotto out of the oven.

4 tablespoons olive oil
1-1/2 pounds of winter squash, cleaned and cut in ½ inch cubes
3 cups veggie broth
1 tablespoon chopped fresh sage
1 cup chopped onion
3 garlic cloves, minced
1 cup uncooked Arborio rice
1/3 cup dried white wine or mirin
1 teaspoon chopped fresh thyme
Sea salt and freshly ground pepper, to taste

Preheat over to 350 degrees F. Place squash on a baking sheet and toss with 2 tablespoons olive oil. Bake at 350 degrees F until squash is tender, about 25-30 minutes. Increase oven temperature to 400 degrees F. Bring broth and sage to a low simmer in a medium saucepan. Heat oil in a large skillet. Sauté onion until it is translucent. Add garlic and rice for about two minutes. Stir in squash, broth mixture, wine, thyme, salt and pepper. Cook about 5 minutes, stirring constantly.

Place the rice mixture in a 9 x13-inch baking dish and bake for about 30 minutes. Stir gently and serve.

Swiss Chard and Rice Noodles

1 tablespoon olive oil
3 garlic cloves, minced
2 teaspoons chopped fresh ginger
1 pound Swiss chard, cut crosswise into 1/2 inch strips, washed and drained
2 tablespoons soy sauce (gluten free)
8 ounces rice noodles
Freshly ground pepper
Crushed red pepper

Heat the oil in a large sauté pan. Add the garlic and ginger and stir over medium heat until beginning to brown, about 2 minutes. Add the chard and the soy sauce and stir to mix. Cover the pan and continue cooking until the chard is wilted and tender, about 20 minutes.

Meanwhile, bring a large pot of water to a boil. Add the noodles and cook until tender, about 3 minutes. Drain, reserving 1/2 cup liquid. Stir the reserved liquid into the chard and divide the noodles among four bowls.

Spoon the chard and its juices over the noodles. Sprinkle the peppers to taste. Serve immediately.

Roasted Veggie Fajitas

2 tablespoons olive oil
3 bell peppers, stemmed, seeded and cut into thin strips
¼ jalapeno pepper, chopped
2 zucchini or yellow squash, halved lengthwise and cut into thin slices
1 red onion, cut into ½-inch thick slices
4 garlic cloves, chopped
1 tablespoon fresh oregano, chopped
Black pepper, cayenne pepper, and paprika, to taste
3 portabello mushrooms, sliced into long thin strips
12 corn tortillas, warmed
2 cups brown basmati rice, cooked and warmed
1 cup tomato salsa
1 cup guacamole

Preheat oven to 400 degrees F. Coat a large baking pan with one tablespoon of olive oil. Mix peppers, zucchini or squash, onion, garlic, oregano and spices in a large bowl and toss with one tablespoon of olive oil. Transfer to a pan and roast for about 20 minutes. Stir and add mushrooms. Continue to roast for an additional 10 minutes. Remove veggies and transfer to serving bowl. To serve fajitas, place one tortilla in a plate, cover with roasted veggies and top with salsa and guacamole.

Stuffed Acorn Squash

Preheat oven to 375 degrees F. Cut each squash in half through stem end. Scrape out seeds with a spoon. Place cut side down in baking dish with a small amount of water. Cover with foil. Bake until fork easily pierces through the squash, about 40 minutes.

Remove from baking pan and flip squash over to reveal their cavities, which can simply be flavored with a small amount of olive oil, sea salt, and maple syrup. For a full meal stuff with Holiday Forbidden Rice recipe (below), a wild rice stuffing, or simply rice and beans.

Holiday Forbidden Rice

Forbidden rice is purple-black in color and makes quite a presentation when serving your dish!

4 tablespoons of olive oil
1 cup of fresh shitake mushroom caps or wild mushroom mixture
4 medium carrots, chopped
3 celery stalks, chopped
1/3 cup of minced shallots
Sea salt and freshly ground pepper, to taste
4 cups cooked Forbidden Rice (follow package instructions)
1-1/3 cup of fresh orange juice
1-1/3 cup of dried cranberries

Preheat oven to 325 degrees F. In a large skillet heat oil over medium heat, add mushrooms and sauté for one minute. Add carrots, celery, and shallots. Season with salt and pepper; sauté for about 5 minutes. Stir in the rice, orange juice and cranberries. Toss to mix well. Pour into a 9" x 13" baking dish. Cover loosely with tin foil and bake until liquid evaporates, about 35 minutes.

Stuffed Peppers

A dollop of guacamole is delicious on top of peppers stuffed with chili and rice, while a dollop of basil pesto works beautifully on top of peppers stuffed with quinoa and roasted veggies.

3 bell peppers, halved, stemmed and seeded
Your choice of stuffing: rice mixed with veggie chili, quinoa mixed with roasted vegetables, or Holiday Forbidden Rice (above).

Preheat oven to 375 degrees F. Grease a shallow baking dish. Arrange the bell pepper halves in a single layer, cut side up, in a prepared pan. Divide the stuffing mixture evenly among the peppers. Cover with aluminum foil and bake until the peppers are tender, about 45 minutes.

Mexican Stuffed Chilies

8 large poblano chilies, more or less depending on size
5 tablespoons of olive oil
3 large garlic cloves, minced
½ cup red onion, finely diced
1 cup bell pepper, diced
1 tablespoon fresh oregano
Sea salt and freshly ground pepper, to taste
1-1/2 cups dried quinoa, cooked (follow package directions)
1/3 cup chopped flat leaf parsley or cilantro
¼ cup fresh lime juice
2 cups fresh salsa

Preheat oven 425 degrees F. Slice chiles lengthwise, remove seeds, and leave stems intact. Brush chiles with olive oil and place on baking sheet. Bake until chiles begin to char. Remove from oven, cool and peel skin. Reduce oven temperature to 350 degrees F.

Heat olive oil in a skillet. Add garlic, onion, bell peppers, oregano, salt and pepper. Sauté for 5 minutes. Stir in quinoa, herbs, lime juice and 1 cup of salsa, remove from heat. Pour remaining 1 cup of salsa at the bottom of a 9 x 13 baking dish. Stuff each chili with the quinoa mixture and place on salsa-lined baking dish. Bake 25 minutes. To serve, sprinkle with salsa.

Stir-fried Veggies

What can be better than stir fry night? Collect a basket of just-picked veggies. Then bring them in, clean them, and start chopping your way to a simple and healthy dinner. The more the merrier!

First, create a simple stir-fry sauce:

¼ cup tamari
1 cup water
3 cloves garlic, minced
1 tablespoon chopped ginger
2 tablespoons sesame oil
1 tablespoon apple cider vinegar
2 tablespoons corn starch

Combine and whisk all ingredients.

Next, cut veggies and line the veggies up in bowls with hard vegetables cooking the longest and soft veggies or greens cooking the shortest amount of time.

2 tablespoons olive oil
1 medium onion, chopped
2 cups of broccoli and/or cauliflower florets
1 cup carrots, sliced thin
2 medium bell peppers, chopped
1 jalapeno, chopped, optional
1 zucchini, cut into 1-inch pieces
1 pound baby bella mushrooms, sliced
4 cups baby greens
4 cloves fresh garlic, chopped, optional
½ cup pineapple, optional

Add oil to a wok and heat. Add all or some of these veggies, plus many other varieties, harder veggies first. Stir-frying each set of veggies for about 3-4 minutes before adding the softer veggies. Once all vegetables are cooked, quickly whisk sauce and pour over veggies. Stir gently several times and serve immediately over organic brown basmati long grain rice or rice noodles.

Summer Grilled Veggie Kabobs

½ cup extra virgin olive oil
¼ cup white wine or mirin
¼ cup lemon juice
Zest of one lemon
2 tablespoons fresh oregano, chopped
1 medium head of garlic, peeled and chopped

Whisk above ingredients to create a marinade.

2 bell peppers of different colors, sliced
1 pint cherry tomatoes
1 Vidalia onion, cut lengthwise
16 oz. baby bella mushrooms, cleaned
1 medium zucchini, yellow squash or patty pan squash, cut into 2 inch chunks
(Add any other available veggies to grill)

Slide vegetables on skewers; brush well with marinade. Grill for 4-5 minutes on each side over medium-hot heat. Continually baste with marinade while grilling.

Tomato, Basil, and Arugula Pasta Salad

4 large tomatoes cut into 1/2-inch dice
3 cloves garlic, minced or pressed
1 cup (packed) arugula leaves (or substitute with other greens)
3 tablespoons shredded fresh basil leaves
Crushed red pepper
2-1/2 tablespoons balsamic vinegar
1/3 cup olive oil
Sea salt and freshly ground pepper
1/2 pound wheat-free penne

Toss the tomatoes, garlic, arugula, basil, crushed pepper, vinegar, oil, salt and pepper to taste in a large serving bowl. Set aside to marinade at room temperature for at least one hour or up to three hours.

Cook the penne al dente, drain briefly, and add to the tomato mixture.

A Vegetable Antipasto!

Imagine your guests arriving on a hot and humid summer afternoon. With a little bit of advanced planning, you can simply pull colorful bowls of all sizes brimming with veggies right out of your refrigerator and fill your table with succulent creations— roasted peppers—Italian-style, Mediterranean olives, a medley of marinated vegetables, a tangy three bean salad, the freshest beets pulled from your garden and seasoned mushrooms. Instead of turning on your oven, create this delicious antipasto. What a meal!

Roasted Peppers

6 colorful peppers, halved and cleaned
¼ cup olive oil

6 cloves of garlic, minced
¼ cup balsamic vinegar
Handful of fresh basil
Sprig of fresh oregano
Sea salt and freshly ground pepper

Preheat oven to 425 degrees F. Place peppers in a bowl and mix with olive oil. Place on baking sheet and bake until black on edges. Cool and remove skin. Place them in a bowl and season with remaining ingredients. Add extra olive oil as needed.

Mediterranean Olives

½ cup olive oil
1 teaspoon red pepper flakes
Grated zest of a lemon
1 teaspoon dried thyme
1 teaspoon dried rosemary
3 garlic cloves, sliced thinly
2 cups mix of green and black olives
3 tablespoons fresh Italian parsley, chopped

Heat olive oil, red pepper flakes, lemon zest, thyme, rosemary and garlic in a pan until it comes to a simmer. Add olives for one minute. Completely cool and transfer into bowl, then chill overnight. When ready to serve, mix well with parsley.

Giardiniera

These mixed pickled vegetables, usually found on an Italian table, are a must when serving an antipasto.

2 cups cider vinegar
½ cup water
2 tablespoons maple syrup, Florida Crystals or other sweetener
1 tablespoon sea salt
1 teaspoon black peppercorns
1 teaspoon mustard seeds
1 teaspoon dried dill
1 cup red bell pepper strips
1 cup diagonally sliced carrots
2 cups small cauliflower florets
2 cups asparagus tips
2 cups trimmed green beans
6 garlic cloves, halved

Simmer the first seven ingredients in a medium saucepan for about five minutes. Place remaining ingredients in a bowl. Pour hot mixture over vegetables and refrigerate overnight, turning occasionally. Remove vegetables from bowl with slotted spoon and serve.

The Freshest Beets

About a dozen beets, cleaned, trimmed, with greens reserved for a salad
1 cup of Garden Vinaigrette

Cook in boiling water until tender. Cool and peel. Cut in quarters. Drizzle Garden Vinaigrette over beets, mix well and refrigerate until serving.

Garlicky Mushrooms

2 pounds of mixed mushrooms
½ cup olive oil
3 garlic cloves, pressed
1 tablespoon chopped fresh flat-leaf parsley
1 tablespoon chopped fresh rosemary
¼ cup white wine vinegar
Sea salt and freshly ground pepper

Place mushrooms and oil in a fry pan over medium heat and constantly turn until mushrooms are tender. Add garlic, parsley, and rosemary until garlic is lightly golden and rosemary is fragrant. Transfer to a bowl and sprinkle with vinegar, salt and pepper.

Sautéed Greens

3 tablespoons of extra virgin olive oil
4 medium garlic cloves, minced
2 pounds of Swiss Chard, Kale or other hearty greens, stem ends discarded and washed well but not dried
Sea salt and freshly ground pepper

In a large pan heat oil over medium heat, add garlic and cook for one minute. Add greens, reduce heat, cover and cook about 5 minutes or until leaves are wilted. Season with salt and pepper.

Four Bean Salad

1 cup dried black beans
1 cup dried dark red kidney beans
1 cup dried chick peas
1 cup balsamic vinegar
1-1/2 tablespoon grainy brown mustard
1 cup extra virgin olive oil
Sea salt and freshly ground pepper
1 lb. green beans, trimmed and cut into 1-1/2 inch pieces
1 medium red onion, chopped
3 tablespoon fresh mint, chopped
3 tablespoon fresh Italian parsley, chopped

Rinse dried beans and soak in plenty of water for about two hours, keeping the three types of beans separated. Drain and bring to boil in three separate pans, all beans completely covered with water. Drain beans when soft but still firm—between 40-60 minutes. Combine all beans in one bowl. Add salt and pepper to taste.

Whisk vinegar, mustard and olive oil. Drizzle over beans and lightly toss. Steam green beans until tender in pot half full of boiling water. Drain and cool.

Add green beans, onion and herbs to the cooled beans. Toss and serve or chill immediately.

Bowl of Antipasto

This "one bowl" antipasto is simple fare throughout the year, making an appearance at a summer picnic or a winter holiday.

3 cups asparagus tips
3 cups broccoli florets
3 cups quartered mushrooms
2 cups colorful bell pepper strips
1 cup pitted Kalamata olives
2 cups garbanzo beans, cooked
5 garlic cloves, minced
½ cup cider vinegar
¼ cup extra virgin olive oil
A handful of fresh basil and Italian parsley, chopped
1 tablespoon of fresh oregano, chopped
Sea salt and freshly ground pepper

Steam asparagus for 3 minutes, covered. Drain and quickly place into ice water. Steam broccoli for 2 minutes, covered. Drain and quickly place into ice water. Combine all ingredients in a bowl and stir gently.

Side Dishes

Oven-roasted Asparagus

3 garlic cloves, halved
2 pounds asparagus spears
2 tablespoons extra virgin olive oil
½ teaspoon dried thyme
Sea salt and freshly ground pepper

Preheat oven to 400 degrees F. Snap off tough ends of asparagus. Add asparagus and garlic to a 9 x 13 baking dish. Drizzle with oil, thyme, salt and pepper, and toss gently. Bake for 20 minutes, stirring once.

Garlic-infused Brussels Sprouts

2 pounds Brussels sprouts, ends trimmed
¼ cup olive oil
15 garlic cloves, peeled and quartered length-wise
2 tablespoons maple syrup
2 tablespoons apple cider vinegar
Sea salt and freshly ground pepper, to taste

Chop Brussels sprouts until coarsely shredded. Heat oil in a large skillet over medium-low heat. Add garlic and sauté until light golden. Add Brussels sprouts, maple syrup, and salt and pepper. Cook five minutes or until lightly browned, stirring constantly. Add 1 cup of water and cook until most of the water has evaporated. Stir in vinegar. Serve immediately.

Lemony-Walnut Brussels Sprouts

2 pounds Brussels sprouts, trimmed and quartered
4 tablespoons walnut oil
2 tablespoons minced shallots
1 teaspoon freshly grated lemon zest
1 tablespoon lemon juice
2 teaspoons whole grain mustard
Sea salt and freshly ground pepper

Steam Brussels sprouts for about 8 minutes or until tender. Place in a serving bowl. Combine and whisk remaining ingredients. Pour over Brussels sprouts and toss gently.

Red Cabbage, German style

1 medium-sized red onion, sliced
1 small head of red cabbage, thinly sliced
½ teaspoon of fennel seeds
½ cup apple juice
2 tablespoons of apple cider vinegar
2 Granny Smith apples
Sea salt and freshly ground pepper

Combine all ingredients except the apples in a large saucepan. Cover and cook over medium heat, stirring occasionally, until vegetables are soft. Reduce heat and stir in apple slices. Cover and cook for about 15 minutes, stirring occasionally. Serve hot.

Easiest Carrots

¼ cup olive oil
1 medium onion, chopped
10 large carrots, peeled and sliced on the diagonal, ½ inch thick
1 tablespoon maple syrup
Sea salt and freshly ground pepper

Warm oil in a large frying pan. Add onion and sauté until soft. Add carrots and sauté until crisp and tender about 17 minutes. Pour in maple syrup and stir well. Season with salt and pepper to taste. Serve immediately.

Carrots and Parsnips

¼ cup olive oil
1-1/2 cup sliced leeks, rinsed well
8 large carrots, peeled and sliced on the diagonal, ½ inch thick
8 parsnips, peeled and sliced on the diagonal, ½ inch thick
Sea salt and freshly ground pepper

Warm oil in a large frying pan. Add leeks and sauté until soft. Add carrots and parsnips and sauté until crisp and tender about 17 minutes. Season with salt and pepper to taste. Serve immediately.

Lemon-Dill Carrots

2 teaspoons olive oil
4 cups diagonally cut carrots
1/3 cup veggie broth
2 teaspoon grated lemon rind
1 tablespoon fresh lemon juice
Sea salt and freshly ground pepper
1 tablespoon fresh dill

Heat the olive oil in a large non-stick skillet over medium heat. Add carrots and sauté for three minutes. Stir in broth, lemon rind and juice, salt and pepper. Cover, reduce heat and cook for about 8 minutes, stirring occasionally. Remove from heat and stir in dill.

Tangy Cauliflower

1 head cauliflower, cut into florets
2 teaspoons Dijon mustard
2 tablespoons balsamic vinegar
2 tablespoons extra virgin olive oil
2 green onions, chopped
3 tablespoons minced fresh dill
Sea salt and freshly ground pepper

Steam cauliflower florets in a medium saucepan until tender crisp; drain. In a mixing bowl, whisk remaining ingredients well. Place cauliflower in a serving bowl. Add dressing and gently stir.

Roasted Broccoli and Cauliflower

8 cups of broccoli and cauliflower florets, combined
¼ cup olive oil
1 head of garlic, peeled and chopped
Sea salt and freshly ground pepper, to taste

Preheat oven to 375 degrees F. Combine all ingredients in a shallow baking dish. Gently stir to cover veggies in olive oil. Bake at 375 degrees F until veggies are tender and tops are browned about 40 minutes. Stir once after 20 minutes in the oven.

Celeriac and Apples

2 pounds celeriac (celery root), peeled and cut into chunks
3 large apples, cored and cut into chunks
1 onion, coarsely chopped
½ cup veggie broth or coconut milk
¼ cup maple syrup
¼ teaspoon cinnamon
½ teaspoon nutmeg

In a large pot bring two inches water to a boil. Add the celery root, apples and onion. Steam covered for about 25 minutes or until very tender. Using a blender, food processor or potato masher, create a puree with the celery root mixture. Stir in and mash remaining ingredients.

Simple Pac Choi

Use as little or as much pac choi as you have for a simple slow cooker side dish.

2 tablespoons tamari
2 tablespoon mirin
2 tablespoons water
1 tablespoon olive oil
2 garlic cloves, minced
2 teaspoons minced fresh ginger
1 large head or 2-3 small heads of pac choi

In a small bowl, combine tamari, mirin and water. Set slow cooker to high. Spread the oil on the bottom of your slow cooker. Sprinkle bottom of cooker with garlic and ginger. Place pac choi evenly in slow cooker and then pour tamari mixture over pac choi. Cook for about 4-1/2 hours on a low setting.

Sautéed Greens

3 tablespoons of extra virgin olive oil
4 medium garlic cloves, minced
2 pounds of Swiss chard, kale or other hearty greens, stem ends discarded and washed well but not dried
Sea salt and freshly ground pepper

In a large pan heat oil over medium heat. Add garlic and cook for one minute. Add greens, reduce heat, cover and cook about 5 minutes or until leaves are wilted. Season with salt and pepper.

Toss with pasta or serve over brown rice for a more substantial meal.

Risotto with Greens

1 medium onion, finely chopped
2 tablespoons olive oil
1 cup risotto, uncooked
2-3 large handfuls of collard greens, kale, spinach, beet greens or any other cooking greens
4 garlic cloves, finely chopped
28 ounces veggie broth
2 quick shakes of red pepper flakes
Sea salt and freshly ground pepper

Sauté onion in olive oil in a medium saucepan. Add risotto and sauté one minute. Add greens and garlic and sauté until greens have wilted. Stir in half of veggie broth. Cook on low heat until most of the liquid is absorbed, stirring consistently. Add the remaining veggie broth and continue to stir. Add spices before serving.

Balsamic Spinach

1 cup balsamic vinegar
½ cup extra virgin olive oil
A handful of basil leaves, chopped
8 cups of spinach, washed well
Sea salt and freshly ground pepper

Simmer vinegar in a small saucepan until slightly reduced. Add olive oil and basil. Lower heat and set aside. Place wet spinach in large saucepan on medium heat and cover. Spinach will wilt quickly. Remove spinach from heat and drain. Place on a platter, season with salt and pepper and drizzle balsamic mixture over spinach.

Green Beans and Garlic

2 pounds of green beans
3 tablespoons of olive oil
2 cloves of garlic, minced
Sea salt and freshly ground pepper

Steam beans for five minutes and then immerse in cold water to stop the cooking process. Drain. In a frying pan warm olive oil. Add beans; stir to coat. Add garlic. Stir and toss for one minute. Remove from heat and season with sea salt and pepper.

Pea Greens

1/2 tablespoon olive oil
6 garlic cloves, minced
1/4 cup vegetable broth
All your pea shoots, chopped about 1"
Sea salt to taste

In large skillet, heat olive oil over medium heat. Add garlic, toss well to coat. Add broth. Cover and cook, stirring occasionally for 5-6 minutes until garlic begins to soften. Remove cover, turn up heat to high, and add pea shoots. Cover and let shoots wilt for 5-7 minutes, stirring frequently and adding one tablespoon of broth at a time to maintain moisture. Remove cover and turn up heat so that all the juices are completely absorbed.

Lemony Sugar Snap Peas

If you are not eating them raw, straight from the garden, or adding them into a summer stir-fry, then try this simple recipe.

2 pounds sugar snap peas, rinsed, dried, tips of the ends cut off, strings removed
3 tablespoons olive oil
3 garlic cloves, peeled and minced
Zest of one lemon
Juice of one lemon
Sea salt and freshly ground pepper

Steam peas in a medium saucepan until tender crisp. Remove immediately and plunge into ice water to stop the cooking process. In a skillet, heat olive oil and add garlic. Add peas and heat quickly, stir-frying. Add the lemon zest, lemon juice, flavor with salt and pepper.

Minty Snow Peas

4 tablespoons olive oil
1 pound sugar snow peas, rinsed, dried, tips of the ends cut off, strings removed
4 cloves garlic, minced
1/2 cup pine nuts
10 large mint leaves, chopped

Heat olive oil in a large skillet on medium high heat. Add the snow peas, garlic, and pine nuts. Stir to coat with the oil. Cook for 1-2 minutes, stirring. Do not overcook the snow peas. They should still be slightly crunchy. Remove from heat. Stir in the chopped mint leaves. Serve immediately.

Roasted Kohlrabi

1-1/2 pounds fresh kohlrabi, ends trimmed, thick green skin sliced off with a knife, diced
1 tablespoon olive oil
1 tablespoon garlic, chopped
Sea salt
White wine vinegar

Set oven to 425 degrees F. Toss the diced kohlrabi with olive oil, garlic and salt in a bowl. Spread evenly on a rimmed baking sheet and put into oven and roast for 30—35 minutes, stirring every five minutes after, for about 20 additional minutes. Sprinkle with vinegar.

Roasted Onions

4 Vidalia or other sweet onion, peeled and sliced into wedges
¼ cup olive oil
1 teaspoon dried rosemary
1 teaspoon dried thyme
Sea salt

Preheat oven to 350 degrees F. Place onions on a baking sheet. Brush onions with olive oil and sprinkle with rosemary, thyme and sea salt. Bake for 30 minutes. Turn onions over once and bake an additional 20 minutes.

Mashed Potatoes

5 pounds Yukon gold potatoes, peeled and quartered
4 cloves of garlic, chopped
6 tablespoons extra-virgin olive oil
¼ cup almond milk, warmed
¼ cup "butter", soy and dairy free
1 teaspoon dried oregano
Sea salt and freshly ground pepper

Bring a saucepan 2/3 full of lightly salted water to a boil. Add the potatoes and garlic until potatoes are tender when pierced with a fork, about 25 minutes.

Drain the potatoes and garlic and return them to pan. Mash potatoes with potato masher, add remaining ingredients, stir well. Serve immediately.

Mashed Potatoes and Greens

3 pounds potatoes, scrubbed and quartered
1 bunch of arugula, stemmed and cleaned (or alternatively baby spinach)
1 cup veggie broth or unsweetened coconut milk beverage
Sea salt and freshly ground pepper
3 tablespoons chopped fresh chives

Bring a saucepan 2/3 full of lightly salted water to a boil. Add potatoes, cover and steam until tender, about 25 minutes, and then drain. Cut the arugula leaves into small strips. In a large bowl, mash the potatoes with the broth or coconut milk and the salt and pepper. Finally stir in the greens and the chives.

Simple Fresh Herb Potatoes

2 lbs. Yukon Gold potatoes, cut into 1 inch pieces
½ cup chopped Italian flat-leaf parsley
½ cup chopped chives
4 tablespoons of olive oil
Sea salt and freshly ground pepper, to taste

Steam potatoes for about 20 minutes or until tender. Transfer to bowl and toss with remaining ingredients.

Turnips and Pears

1 lb. turnips
3 pears
2 tablespoons olive oil
1 onion, peeled and sliced thinly
2/3 cup walnuts, halved
Sea salt and freshly ground pepper, to taste
1/2 lemon
Fresh chopped parsley

Cut turnip in half, then into 1/4 inch thick slices. Cut pears in half, core and cut into 1/4 inch thick slices. Saute turnips in olive oil until tender and crisp. Add pears and onions. Cook while stirring mixture for about 3 minutes. Add walnuts. Cook for 2 minutes. Season with salt and pepper. Squeeze lemon over mixture and sprinkle with parsley.

Turnip Fries

Turnips, peeled and chopped into French-fry strips
Olive oil
Sea salt

Lightly coat turnip strips with olive oil. Place on a flat baking sheet and sprinkle with sea salt. If desired, also sprinkle with your favorite herbs and spices. Bake in a 350 degrees F for 20 minutes.

Roasted Sweets and Beets

5 large sweet potatoes, peeled and cut into 2 inch pieces
6 large beets, peeled and cut into 2 inch pieces (reserve beet greens for salad)
1 medium onion, chopped
1/3 cup olive oil
2 teaspoons freshly ground pepper
1 tablespoon garlic powder

Mix all ingredients well in a bowl and transfer to a shallow baking dish. Bake on 400 degrees F, mixing twice during baking, for about 40 minutes or when veggies are soft and caramelized.

Maple Sweet Potato Casserole

1 tablespoon olive oil
3 pounds of sweet potatoes, shredded
¼ cup maple syrup
1/3 cup unsweetened shredded coconut
¼ teaspoon ground cinnamon
1 cup fresh chopped pineapple

Lightly oil slow cooker. Add sweet potatoes, maple syrup, coconut and cinnamon. Cover and cook on low for about 5 hours. Stir in pineapple and cook an additional 20 minutes. Alternatively, bake in oven on 350 degrees F for 35 minutes. Add pineapple and bake an additional 5 minutes.

Sweet Potato Chips

5 sweet potatoes
¼ cup of olive oil
1 teaspoon of sea salt

Preheat oven to 400 degrees F. Cut potatoes in 1/8-inch thick slices. Pour olive oil on the bottom of a baking sheet and spread evenly. Place one layer of potato slices on baking sheet and sprinkle with salt. Bake for 12 to 14 minutes, turning once. Remove and cool.

Squash, Pear, Cranberry Bake

1 butternut squash, peeled, cleaned and cut into 1-inch chunks
4 pears, peeled, cored and sliced
2 cups dried cranberries
1 onion, chopped
½ cup maple syrup
2 tablespoons cinnamon
1 teaspoon nutmeg
½ cup olive oil

Preheat oven 375 degrees F. Combine all ingredients in a shallow baking dish. Stir well allowing the olive oil and maple syrup to coat all ingredients. Bake for about 45 minutes or until squash is tender and caramelized. Stir occasionally.

Winter Squash Casserole

6 cups cooked squash or pumpkin, mashed or pureed
1 cup coconut milk
1 cup maple syrup, divided into two ½ cups
1 cup gluten-free whole oats
¼ cup olive oil, plus one tablespoon

Preheat oven to 375 degrees F. Mix oats, ½ cup maple syrup and ¼ cup olive oil into a small bowl and set aside. Spread one tablespoon of olive oil in a baking dish. Mix squash, coconut milk, and remaining maple syrup in a bowl and spoon gently into the baking dish. Top with oats mixture. Bake for 25 minutes or until squash is hot throughout and oat mixture is browned. (Cover with tin foil if topping begins to brown quickly.)

Index

Julie Sochacki is a cook and gardener who is passionate about local, high-quality ingredients and healthy eating. She strongly believes in local and sustainable community farms and wants to spread the word about the benefits of cooking with fresh, simple ingredients. www.juliecooksbliss.com

Jason Houston is a photographer and filmmaker focused on social and environmental issues. He has been photographing the local, sustainable agriculture and the food system for over a decade. www.jasonhouston.com